ABOUT THE AUTHOR

Meet Gaurinanadhana P S, a bright and imaginative young poet who began writing poems at the age of nine. With a vivid imagination and a love for words, Gaurinandhana finds inspiration in the world around her from the rustling leaves in her backyard to the stars twinkling in the night sky. Now, at just eleven years old, she is excited to share her first book, which features twenty of her heartfelt poems.

Gaurinandhana believes that poetry is a magical way to express feelings and ideas. She loves to explore different themes, from friendship and nature to dreams and adventures. When she's not writing, you can find her reading her favorite books, drawing colorful pictures, or playing with her pet, Kannan, a grey parrot.

Through her poetry, Gaurinandhana hopes to inspire other kids to discover their own voices and express themselves creatively. She can't wait for you to dive into her collection and experience the beauty of her words!

English Language
Journey of My Wonder World
(Poems)
by
Gaurinandhana Sushil

♦

Published in November 2024
by Kairali Books Private Limited
Thalikkavu Road, Kannur.
Ph : 0497-2761200
E-Mail : kairalibooksknr@gmail.com

♦

Illustrations & Cover Design
Smitha K E

♦

74/24-25/Sl.No.1641/100/NS.18.6
ISBN 978-93-5973-770-6

Journey of My Wonder World

Gaurinandhana Sushil

Kairali Books

Forward

It is with great honour and pride that I introduce The Journey of My Wonder world , the debut anthology by Gaurinandhana Sushil, a promising student in Grade 5 at our school, Metropolitan International Indian School. Gaurinandhana Sushil has demonstrated a remarkable ability to express her thoughts, imaginations and emotions in a way that captivates readers across all age groups.

Her anthology reflects not only the purity and curiosity of childhood but also an impressive depth of insight for someone so young. Through her eloquent verses, Gaurinandhana reveals a unique perspective on the world, transforming the ordinary into something remarkable and filled with wonder.

As the Principal, it has been a privilege to observe her development, both as a student and as an emerging budding poet. Her creativity, dedication, and passion for writing are commendable, and they offer a glimpse into the bright future that lies ahead of her. I am confident that The Journey of My Wonder World will mark the beginning of an extraordinary literary path.

On behalf of the school community, I extend my heartfelt congratulations to Gaurinandhana on this remarkable achievement and wish her continued success in all her future endeavors. May her poetry inspire many more to pursue their talents with the same commitment and enthusiasm.

With Regards
Dr. Abdul Majeed
Principal
Metropolitan International Indian School

Message

It is a rare and beautiful moment when a young mind opens the door to creativity and invites us into a world filled with wonder and imagination. Gaurinandhana Sushil, a Grade 5 student at Metropolitan International Indian School, has done just that with her debut anthology The Journey of My Wonder World In these pages, we witness the unfolding of a talent that is both tender and profound, one that reflects the purity of childhood alongside the quiet wisdom of someone far beyond her years.

Gaurinandhana has an extraordinary ability to capture the fleeting beauty of everyday life and transform it into something timeless. Her words flow with a natural grace, drawing us into her reflections on the world around her, where even the smallest moments become a source of inspiration. There is a gentle rhythm to her poetry, a music that resonates in the hearts of her readers, speaking of innocence, curiosity, and an unquenchable thirst for understanding.

As Vice Principal, it has been a privilege to witness Gaurinandhana's journey. She is a student whose passion for writing is as inspiring as it is promising. The Journey of My Wonder is not only a celebration of her growth as a poet but also a testament to her bright and boundless future. I have no doubt that this anthology is just the beginning of a remarkable literary path, one that will continue to shine with the same brilliance and wonder she so effortlessly shares.

With heartfelt congratulations and best wishes for her continued success,

Ms. Nancy K Anto
Vice Principal
Metropolitan International Indian School

Message

Teaching Gauri has been a wonderful experience, and it is with great pride that I witness her artistic expression in The Journey of My Wonder world ."Her poems reflect not only her creativity but also a deep sensitivity and insight that is rare at such a young age.

Gauri's ability to weave words into beautiful imagery speaks to her natural gift for storytelling, and I am certain this is only the beginning of a bright literary journey. May her talent continue to blossom as she discovers new horizons in her writing.

With heartfelt congratulations,

Ansila
Arabic Teacher
Metropolitan International Indian School

Review

'Nature is not a place to visit.
It is Home'

The journey of my world is a compilation of 20 poems created by our talented student Gourinandhana Sushil of Metropolitan International Indian School,Ajman. It takes readers on a thrilling journey along with a cluster of wonders which she observed with her family from nature.

Each line in the poems has its own beauty and magic that makes the readers elated and it shows the true majesty of our Earth. She was deeply connected by the different forms and creations of nature. The beautiful sound of drizzling rain drops, and the smell of nature shifts readers to a world of imagination. All these beauties created a soothing feeling that made her delighted.

It has been an honor to be your teacher and witness your growth. Keep exploring and Best Wishes for a successful and flourshing future!

With Best Wishes
Girija Murali
Teacher
Metropolitan International Indian School, Ajman

Message

The collection of poems 'The Journey of my Wonder World' by Gourinandhana. I love this collection of peoms! Truely inspiring. I especially like the way you express yourself through the feelings you experienced in your life. Overall, your poem effectively captures the transition of day into night and the excitement of seeing a rainbow. With some enhancements in language, punctuation, and imagery, it could become even more evocative and engaging. Great work on creating a poem that celebrates the beauty of nature with such simplicity and joy!

Hope Gourinandhana would strengthen her talent through learning. I wish her all the best.

Best Regards,

Susmi
Class Teacher
Metropolitan International Indian School, Ajman

CONTENTS

Wonder Touch

Who is pulling me, there is no one here
I can't go forward, someone pulling my skir
AAHHHHH, it's prickling my fingers,
When I touch it goes to sleep
WOW….. TOUCH TOUCH TOUCH"
AWWWWwwwwww It's not night
Wake up wake up wake up Open your eyes
When I slowly touched it, didn't respond
OOOOHHH It's my mistake sorry
When I pull my dress, it must have hurt the plant
It's my mistake it's my mistake it's my mistake
Bye I'm going, when I turned around
A miracle happened, it came back

It's very beautiful and has purple flowers
I went there and gave it a hug in joy
AAAHHH! My arms hurt and it went to sleep
Surprise it's a
TOUCH ME NOT PLANT
TOUCH WONDER TOUCH TOUCH
WONDER TOUCH

Sky Miracle

One, the "sun" is going to set
Two, the "birds" are going to nest
Three, the "sky" is beginning to dark
Four, the "moon" is starting to shine
Five, the "clouds" are fading to darkness
Six, the "stars" are hidden on there
Seven, the "night" is coming peacefully
Eight, the "rain" is waiting to drop
Nine, the "people" are going to sleep
Ten, I'm waiting for the sun to rise
Because I want to see that beauty
Seven colored sky miracle
Yes yes it's a RAINBOW

Red battalion

Mom
Who bit me?
Ouch, it hurts me so much.
Yes, I get it.
Who are you to bite me?
Your very painful
I will kill you now.
1 2 3 4—too many to count.
Even if I count to ten,
It will not finish.
Oh, it's a row.
Where is it coming from?
I cannot find it.
Ok, I will let you go now.
Mom, where is this coming from?
Dear, there's a fallen tree branch there.
Maybe it's coming from there.
Mom I want to see it.
Oh, I see it.
Where is their home?
Yes. I found it.
But it looks like a bird's nest.
Hundreds, no, thousands of them
Is it in the home?
Mom What's its specialty?
Dear, they always stay together.

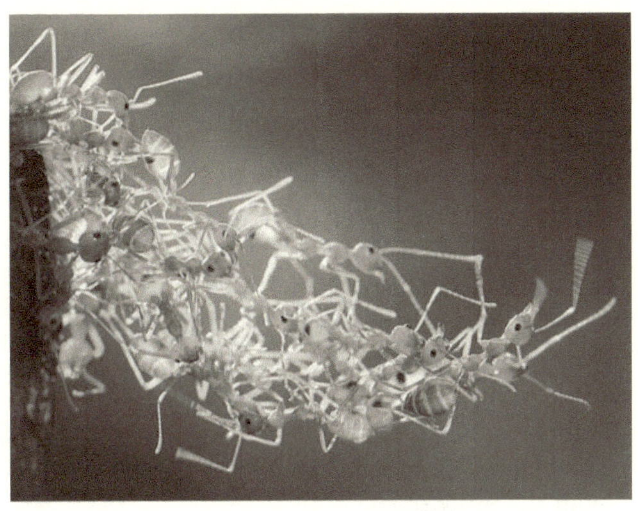

They are never separated from each other.
Yes mom
They are always coming and going together.
These construction workers make beautiful houses.
With leaves
I want to touch Mom.
No, dear, don't touch it.
It's coming....
Phew....
I just escaped it.
It's my fault.
I should not have touched it.

○

Jumbo Beauty

Cling, cling, cling
Yes, he is coming.
The first time I was about to see him
Oh, he looks like a big rock.
Two white pearly tusks
Seeing his tusks, I am scared.
Because it's too sharp.
He has a long trunk with big holes.
It's for breathing.
A long tail with tiny hairs
Small button-like eyes
But his ears are too big.
I gave him some food.
That time, I understood that he took it with his trunk.
How he's chewing
Oh, he has teeth inside.
Oh, he uses his trunk for drinking and bathing.
He has four big leg-like pillars.
But I cannot still understand why his eyes are small.
Dad said if his eyes were big, he could see himself.
He cannot see his eyes because his ears are covering him.
Even if he is the biggest creature, he still can't see himself.
You know the biggest specialty of him.
I have seen him so many times.
But hearing the sound of his chain
You will run to see him.
That's the wonder of an elephant.
Our wonder is sree kuttan.

Unpredictable Hero

I don't know how to explain.
I don't know which word to use to describe
All the words I learned cannot be explained.
When I hold his hand in any dark place,
I will not be afraid.
Mom has told the first person I have called, and that's him.
"If I am tired of walking, he will piggyback me on his shoulder.
Sitting on his shoulder at that time,
I saw the most beautiful vision.
Until this, he has never hit me.
So when he yells at me, it's very painful.
You know what is the saddest thing for me.
I only have a little time to spend with him.
But that time is the most precious thing for me.
I think all of my friends have only a little time
to spend with their heroes.
Because most of the heroes spend their time at work,
The most special thing about this person is that
He never forces me to do anything.
I have never heard him demanding or
complaining about anything.
Because he loves me very much.
I think that every hero is like this.
You know who that hero is.
The one and only person in the
World like that is a father.

○

My peace place

Whoosh.........
Whoosh........
Wow, so cool. It's an awesome feeling.
It's like the leaves are talking to each other.
They are talking so loud.
because there are so many leaves on the grandpa tree.
We need three friends to hug the grandpa tree.
Sitting down near it is another level of positive energy.
Near the place, there is a blackboard tree.
According to ancient belief, it was known as the devil tree.
Because there was a myth that the devil was living there.
All of this is staying inside in one place.
It's temple "All around it is a greenery-like field.
In between them, there are two fish ponds.
With all of this, my favorite thing about this
Is that what makes my mind calm?
That is the specialty of that place.
It's my peaceful place.

○

My first Rain

My first Rain
What is that sound?
I even tried to close my ears.
But it's so annoying.
I asked mom.
What's that sound?
She said to look outside.
Then I saw it was raining.
Oh, it's so much fun.
But then there was thunder.
But it's so much fun playing in the rain
I love rain.

Red and black drops

Red and black drops
RED AND BLACK DROPS
Ouch something pricked my leg.
What is that?
I think my leg got injured.
I want to see what pricked my leg.
Oh no! Is that blood?
There's so much blood.
Wait a minute.
That's not blood.
Oh, all around are these little drops.
Let's pick one of it up.
No, it's not blood.
I took one of them.
Oh, it's not only red.
It's red and black.
What is this?
It's so beautiful.
I have never seen anything like this before.
Where is this coming from?
Oh, it's in a dried pod.
From which tree is it coming from?
I looked everywhere.
I found it. It's a creeper.
It's so high.
Just when I opened the pod

It has so many drops in it.
But the black one is only holding on to the pod.
When I picked it all up in my hand,
It was like I was holding lots of ladybugs.

○

Glass pecker

Tack, tack, tack
Oh, so irritating.
Who is knocking on the door so early?
Tack, tack, tack
Mom, who is at the door,
Tack, tack, tack
Mommm
Who is disturbing me?
It is so loud.
I want to sleep.
Dear, why are you screaming so loud?
Someone is disturbing me.
Oh, you want to know who that is?
Go outside, and you will know.
Yes, I want to know.
Who was disturbing me?

Tack, tack, tack"The sound is getting louder.
Is it any construction work?
No! It's a natural engineer.
Wow, so beautiful.
Oh wow, a red cap, a black and white coat,
and a sharp beak.
Oh, you are the driller.
Mom, it's a woodpecker.
I want to touch you.
Oh, you went away.
I only heard him peck wood.
I don't know why he pecked the glass.
I want to know why he did that.
Dear, what are you doing here?
I want to know why he pecked the glass.
You go stand in front of the window.
You can see your reflection.
Yes, yes, yes, I can see my reflection.
Can he see his reflection?
Is that why, mom?
He thinks that it's his enemy.
Oh, to hear this much sound, his beak
must be sharp.
Was he a smart natural engineer?
It's not a woodpecker.
It's. a glass pecker.

o

Beats of My Heart

Beep, Beep, Beep
Can you hear that sound?
Yes! We can, but we can't see.
Oh! When the sound stops, we will die.
You know, the only thing in our lives like
that is our "mother."
Like our hearts are purifying blood

Our "mother" rectifies our character.
In fact, without us saying anything
She knows our movements and what we want.
If we make a mistake, she will shout at you.
But it's for our goodness.
From morning until night,
she repeats the time every day.
Still, I don't know why she does that.
Oh, no, sometimes it's irritating.
But if she stops all of this,
We can't even think of that.
When the beat stops, it's like I'm dead.
Wherever I go, I want my mother, like my heart beats.

○

Chinese violet

Oh wow
In a drop of water
It will explode
The first time
I have saw it
Is in a hand
When the hand opened
It was like a grain
When my uncle introduced me it
I didn't know that
This was a natural fireworks
When I took it
I put some water on it
It exploded
This is an awsome thing
I want to know where it came from
I searched everywhere in the field
But then I found it Inside the plants
it was in the mud with the other plants
Oh it was this beautiful
It has violet flowers
It has manys crackers inside it
Oh it's green too
I want one green
But there's no water
Mom what do I do

It Is also called saliva cracker
So you can use your saliva
Oh mom it's no working
Raw ones don't crack
You can use the other one
Oh yes yes
It's cracking mom
a purple flower with crackers
This another beauty of nature

○

Flying Inspector

In a morning
Is the first time
I have saw him
Sunrise hitting the field
Him sitting there thinking
I went near him
But he slowly got up
And went to the feild
Then he started thinking again
But on one leg
Suddenly he took something
And flew away
Oh he was not thinking about something
He was thinking about food
But I wonder
why he stood on one leg
Oh he catched a fish
Mom I couldn't see him closely
Dear he will come in the evening
But I saw him before evening
He was in the front of our house
He has no fear
When the JCB came
And was removing the dirt
He was walking there peacefully
I wondered

What he was doing there
Once he was standing on the gate
Then he gets down
To go near the JCB
Again, again and again
What is he doing
He is like a inspector
Slowly slowly I went near him
But he was still inspection the work
Then gone the coconut tree
I thought he was going
But suddenly
He went down near the mud
Searching again
Then something was in his beak
It's a worm
Oh he is not thinking
he is searching for food
I love white flying inspector

O

Eventide

Come guys let's sit here
To enjoy the Beauty of it
In my house
It has special place Upstairs
Sitting there we can see
Nature's beauty
We can hear songs from the temple
Bird are flying to their nests
that time the peacocks are coming to the feild

They are walking lazyly
They are also playing hide and seek
So are so many kids playing football
In the feild side
So many people watering the crops
Night is coming
The sun is falling
If you walk outside
A cold breeze will touch you and go
If you walk slowly
You can see the beauty of the place
In the lights of chirath
The temple and banyan tree is like heaven
See all of this is the most precious thing
You can ever wish for.

○

Jumper's visit

Oh no
Who jumped beside me
Who is here at this time rainy night
Oh it's you who startled me
You are so beautiful
Mom we got a visitor
A visitor who has startled me
Where are you coming from
Mom I want to where lives
Let's go there now
Dear it's night time
Let's go tomorrow
Mom it's so small
Dear it has three stages
First it's an egg

Second it's a fish
Third it's this form
Why is it here mom at this time
Dear it because we live near a field
And also there are insects here
Oh you little jumper
You only came for food right
I hate your music
But still you came to visit me
I like you

○

Miraculous Drop

Drop drop drop Mom telling drop
What's that Cool drop
First time I saw it I wonder
It's so disgusting
My mom took it and put it on her eye
Oh I think mom went crazy
When I touched all of my thoughts were wrong
Is it a jelly no no no no
It's nothing compared to jelly
It's too soft and cool like ice sticks
I tried putting it on my eye
It was so refreshing

I could not describe it
It's so addicting
I couldn't take it of
I kept it until i reached home
I was so sad when it withered
Now only I understood mom's words
If you get a chance to get one of it
Do not waste that chances.

○

Old and golden pearls

1 2 3 to many to count
I have saw many wonders of nature
Walk walk walk
Walk with nature
In the first step
I saw a natural beauty
But I will still touch it
In the second step
I will see ladybug
But it's not that

It's a coral bead
In the third step
I will see Chinese violet
I searched for the crackers
But can't find it
I saw some people
It's my neighbour
In the fifth step
I will see a hatter beauty
It's a red whiskered bull bull
In the sixth step
I will see a cat tail
Oh it's a plant
Hehehe
It's a congon grass
In the seventh step
I see some dogs playing in the field
In the eighth step
I hear different sweet voices
It's not humans
It's the bird
In the nineth step
I will be holding someone's hand
And walking
That sweet person is my grandma
In the tenth step
Me and my cousin will be running
There will be someone holding something special
That my grandpa
The old and gold pearls of the house

○

Thorny Beauty

When I walk in my garden
Wait where's that smell coming from
So many flowers are there
But which flower is that smell coming from
Let's check ow there's thorns on this flower
Oh it's coming from you
Oh it's so thorny
When I went closer
The smell was irresistible
Oh it's you who was making atractted to the smell
1 2 3 4 5 6 7 8 9 10
To many count

The layers are so beautiful
Like a gown
The bud is a green beauty
When your starting to bloom
Your a reddish beauty
But when you start to wither
Its a sad moment to me
All of layers slowly flying away
Then you will be a stick
Why did god give thorns to a beauty like you
Maybe it's because of your beauty
No can pluck you
Oh god you are very creative

Mischievous Sis

One two
No we are one
you also have a person like that right
She is like a boy
Too ENERGETIC
Always doing gymnastics
Actually she is gifted a great talent of gymnastics from God
Also she is a great dancer
I can't do that but she can
When we go outside

We have our own plans
When we are going to our home country
We don't like to go outside
We want to play in our house
Even in the place we stay
We are very different from each other
She is very active
And also an extrovert
I AM not like that
So we always get into a fight
Some times she is irritating me
She is always willing to make friends
She a lot of friends that me
I am surprised how can she create
a friend group bigger than 10 people
Even from all of this she is a scardey cat
If we see each other we will fight
But if we don't see each other we will be sad
I realised that we she she went to our home country
Because the time we saw each other we were inseparable
She is my cousin
But it's not like that for me
She is like my younger sister
Do you have. PERSON like this
Yeah you might have
every one also have maybe.

○

Memorable Fest

Boom...boom...boom
Oh it's starting now
Mom I want to go there
But it's still dark outside
It's starting this early
Yes dear we can go
But wait for morning
I am very excited
That I can't even sleep
I want to check out
What song am hearing
Dear go get ready now
So we can see it
Mom who is sitting outside
With a clay pot
Is that lady singing a song
You should go sit in front of her
The lady has a Pot with lots of threads

She is also singing a song
Dear it's a ritual for visual impairment
Mom in this day there are many rituals
Yes, all of them are apart of this day
When are we going there
Mom let's go now
Oh there's to many lights
It's decorated with light bulbs
The field is like a market
To many sellers
Mom you told there will be lots of people
But there's only little amount of people
You have to wait until afternoon
Mom when will our relatives arrive
Just when we get home
Doomm, Doomm, Doomm
Mom it's starting now
The drummers are here and elephant are coming
Oh wow there are many people and elephants
Everyone is waiting to watch it
There are lots of sounds
Horns,chains, people, sellers and drummers
Onh mom it's a huge mess
But, I like it
When night comes
In the light
Comes in big group called theyyam
Mom When will this end
It will not finish today it will finish tomorrow morning
It's a funday I got to meet and see lots of people and
sightings
It's a fun and memorable day

○

Natural FASHIONISTA

R - for red   What's that {cheeks}
B - for black What's that { hat }
W - for white What's that {frock}
Br - for brown What's that { coat}
Oh what a natural fashionista
Mhmm mhmm
Who is singing that song in the bush
It's so mesmerising
Where is the sound
What is this seed
Where is it coming from
Oh it's black jamun
Who ate this
Again who is singing
Think he is on the sitting on the tree
To eat the fruit

Oh wait that's him flying to the electricity cord
What a beauty
It's a bird
It's natural fashionista
Did you bring that cap for me
I like it so much
It's made naturally
Will you be my friend
So I can learn your type of fashion
Whenever I dress up
I always remember you
Because your fashion is very stylish